That Is a

By Liza Charlesworth

ISBN: 978-1-339-02779-1

Art Director: Tannaz Fassihi; Designer: Tanya Chernyak
Photos © Getty Images.
Copyright © Liza Charlesworth. All rights reserved. Published by Scholastic Inc.

1 2 3 4 5 6 7 8 9 10   68   32 31 30 29 28 27 26 25 24 23

Printed in Jiaxing, China. First printing, August 2023.

SCHOLASTIC

See the dog with a bone?
This soft bed is its home.
A bed is a nice home for dogs.

A gull chose grass and twigs.
Then, it made a nest on a branch.
A nest is a snug home for chicks.

Do not poke this hive!
A whole lot of bees are inside.
A hive is a bee home.

Who made this home
in the shape of a dome?
Ants did! Lots of them!

These cubs like to doze
in a cave made of stone.
A cave is a fine place to rest.

Dig, dig, dig…POP!
See the mole with a pink nose?
A hole is a safe home for moles!

Dogs and bees and gulls!
Ants and cats and moles!
The globe is so huge
and has lots of homes.